Supplemental Liturgical Materials

Prepared by the
Standing Liturgical Commission

THE CHURCH HYMNAL CORPORATION, NEW YORK

5   4   3   2   1

Contents

"... these things God has revealed to us through the Spirit;
for the Spirit searches everything, even the depths of God."
I Corinthians 2: 10, NRSV

Preface

The subject and study of this book—the language of liturgy—are no longer new for the Episcopal Church. Since the development of the 1979 Book of Common Prayer, sensitivity has grown to the power words and images in worship have to shape our understanding of and relationship with God. Along with this sensitivity has grown the commitment of the church to explore ways to make it possible for its worship to reflect this awareness and become as fully revelatory of the mystery of God and as balanced as possible in speaking of and for God's people.

Three General Conventions of the church (1985, 1988, and 1991) have reflected on and wrestled with these emerging questions and have enacted legislation that affirmed the continuing search toward a faithful and open response. Three publications (*Liturgical Texts for Evaluation*, 1987; *Prayer Book Studies 30: Supplemental Liturgical Texts*, 1989; and the present volume, *Supplemental Liturgical Materials*, 1991) bear witness to two important discoveries from the first five years' work.

First, the principles upon which the studies were originally based have been tested and proved: remaining faithful to the familiar forms of Anglican worship; drawing 'new' prayer material directly from biblical and other traditional texts; seeking balanced rather than 'neutral' language and imagery for speaking of God. Often a delicate course to chart, the effort has resulted in prayers and scriptural texts of depth and substance; not finished 'products,' but still 'works in progress.'

Second, study of these documents will indicate that the five-year process of developing these materials has been a 'conversation' involving the church in a wide range of settings. In addition to providing services and materials for use and study in worship, it has been the Liturgical Commission's commitment to educate about, to respond to, and to guide the emerging dialogue and debate — all essential elements in an endeavor of this kind. Once again, liturgy has shown itself to be the 'work of the people' at many levels.

This book, then, is both the result of and reflection on a maturing dialogue. The Standing Liturgical Commission's hope is that the next phase of the 'conversation' will involve congregations and individuals interested in continuing — or joining — the ongoing process. The invitation is open to all.

A Word on Language

In the evolving conversation, it is particularly important to understand the use of terms. Over the past five to ten years, discussions on language and liturgy have come to be subsumed under the general heading of "inclusive language" — past the time that term accurately described the subject's complexity and subtlety. In the *Supplemental Liturgical Material*, as in previous studies, use of the term "inclusive language" has been deliberately kept to a minimum. Recalling the first principles upon which this study was — and is — based, the better, more accurate term, would be "*balanced* language" — and even then, could be "balanced imagery" as much as "balanced language."

The past decade has recognized an evolution in awareness and understanding of language, which the three stages of the Liturgical Commission's study roughly parallel. It is a process which has moved from, first, a call for the use of "non-sexist" terms, where gender-specific words such as "he" and "man" were replaced with terms such as "God" or "humanity." This stage of the study is documented in *Liturgical Texts for Evaluation* (1987). A second stage has been the use of balanced language which includes both masculine and feminine words, images, and metaphors (*Supplemental Liturgical Texts*, 1989). A third stage which is emerging, depends not on defining itself as "opposed to" or even "different from" traditional means of expression. With metaphor and image as its foundation, this third stage of the study challenges the Church to hear and use familiar and new passages and prayers in a different way. In this phase of the process, language is opened to new interpretation and the hearer to deeper meaning (*Supplemental Liturgical Material*, 1992).

Use of Supplemental Liturgical Materials: Content and Intent

The *content* of this book is directly linked to its two predecessors, though its form is noticeably different. Previous volumes presented the new services in their entirety, to introduce them more easily to worshipping congregations. In this volume, the worship materials are offered as *resources* to supplement existing Rite II services of the *Book of Common Prayer*. After all, the 'conversation' in which the church at large is engaged takes place in a wide range of settings, and in congregations with a wide range of experience with such study. With these materials, each congregation can prepare services suited to their level of preparation and modify their use as familiarity grows.

The first *intent* of this book, then, is to provide optimum flexibility in planning worship with supplemental liturgical materials. A second intent, no less important than the first, is that brief *reference* materials be as easily accessible as possible. Instead of being contained in a separate volume, as before, the educational commentary is here bound together with the new or suggested text. An updated bibliography directs the interested worshipper to further educational resources.

Expanded worship and easier study are central to the effort contained in *Supplemental Liturgical Material*. It is important that those involving themselves with these resources be aware that it will involve some extra thought and preparation to put them into use. These are not "ready made" services, but resources that will require flexibility, time, and a cooperative spirit to put fully into practice.

A Word on Worship

Anglicanism has historically understood worship as the experience of the gathered community. Worship which is formed by the *Book of Common Prayer* makes what would otherwise be an *individual* experience, or experience of a *collection of individuals*, a *common* experience, one "greater than the sum of its parts."

The worship materials contained in this book provide further possibilities for expanded worship, but this is always intended to mean their use *within the structure, scope and context of the Book of Common Prayer*. The shape of common worship, using these materials, should be easily recognizable as "Episcopal". They should display the structure which identifies the liturgies as belonging to our historical common experience, even as they allow for equally important variations in tone and expression. Specifically, the familiar structure of the Daily Office should be evident in services of prayer and reflection on scripture. Similarly, the traditional shape of the Eucharist (the gathering, the proclamation of the Word and the prayers of the people, followed by the fourfold taking, blessing, breaking and giving of bread and wine) should be retained as resources from this volume and from the *Book of Common Prayer* are combined.

Finally and importantly, according to the enabling resolutions at each Convention, these materials are permitted for use "always under the direction of the diocesan bishop or ecclesiastical authority."

Use of Supplemental Liturgical Materials: Cooperative Implementation

Preparing services for worship is always, at its best, a cooperative effort. This will be even more important with a congregation that has decided to involve itself with these materials and their study.

Many stages will be necessary, different in each location. Questions to be considered might be summed up as those helping to determine the "range, frequency, occasion and duration" of use. Which of these materials will assist our prayers? Which are we willing to use now, and which will we try later? How often will we pray with these materials? Which services are best suited to their use — initially, and in the longer run? Are there special occasions or specific groups that might begin earlier, while the congregation as a whole continues study and discussion prior to their participation?

It is not only the questions, but who is involved in discussing them, that is important. There are important pastoral considerations involved in the use of these materials. The establishment of clarity of purpose is vitally important, and should begin with clarity between liturgical leaders and the congregation. This can best be achieved by a process of dialogue that begins with the questions above (among others) and ends with a carefully considered statement of purpose and vision.

Use of Supplemental Liturgical Materials: Range, Frequency, Duration

Range: These materials may be used in an almost infinite variety of ways, from supplementing only the Opening Acclamation of the Eucharist to using materials from each section of the eucharistic text. Likewise, a set of possibilities is available for the Offices. A congregation may choose to use one or more options, and to change the range of use over time as familiarity increases.

An important note in considering the range of use is found in the section which provides "Forms for the eucharistic prayer." In this section, eucharistic prayers being developed in specific communities, or other occasional or written-for-the-occasion prayers, may be used with the Order for Celebrating the Holy Eucharist on pages 400-401 of the *Book of Common Prayer*.

Frequency: Congregations that participated in the last evaluation period found that initial *frequent* use of new prayers facilitated familiarity, which then made possible their more occasional use as part of a regular rotation of services with those in the *Book of Common Prayer*. Now, with even more options available (ie., the use of only specifically chosen sections of the *Materials*, not necessarily the entire service), worship leaders will be able to better determine the best way for their congregation to simultaneously experience new prayers and maintain continuity of community worship life.

Duration: The *Materials* are authorized through the Triennium beginning Advent 1991. There may be particular liturgical seasons when a congregation will pray with them; in other places it will be possible to immediately integrate them into regular worship throughout the year. Without some extended exposure to the prayers, it is less likely that they will be incorporated naturally into a community's life. After the 1985-90 extended evaluation period, participating congregations reported hearing from members that had come to appreciate them and missed the opportunity to pray with them.

Practical Approach: Whatever the range, frequency, and duration of use, the development and printing of worship pamphlets for services will make possible this repeated use without the necessity of repeating their production. Care for the appearance and quality of such "pew pamphlets" will be important in their assisting in (rather than distracting from) worship. Booklets should have a clear typeface, uncluttered graphics and be made of durable materials.

Music and Inclusive Liturgy: In the preparation of *The Hymnal, 1982*, close attention was paid to the issues of inclusivity, but not to the exclusion of all texts failing to meet the criterion of inclusivity. Thus, in planning services with these texts, hymns should be reviewed for their consistency with the setting in which they will be sung. To assist in this task, Appendix C, on page oo contains a list of hymns which are particularly fitting for use in these services and a list of those which will prove less useful.

Congregational Preparation

It has been noted that the process of introducing and using these materials must include adequate consideration of the human dynamic involved in a community at prayer.

Whatever the shape of the local congregational process, it will be important for participants in liturgies utilizing these texts to

- understand the reason for their existence. The background information in this book might be shared with the congregation in an adult forum or as literature sent to the home or available at the church.

- appreciate the options for worship available in the present *Book of Common Prayer*. Use of *Supplemental Liturgical Material* offers an excellent opportunity to open the present prayer book for congregational study. For example, study of and prayer with the two eucharistic prayers in this book, is an excellent way to compare them to the six eucharistic prayers in the Prayer Book and discuss the different emphases in each. *The Supplemental Materials* can lead to a deeper understanding and appreciation of the Episcopal Church's heritage of worship, upon which this book builds.

- benefit from the commentary on the texts included in this book. Providing opportunities for participants to study the texts and commentary, with prayer books and bibles will raise the level of community and individual participation.

One approach for the study of the *Supplemental Liturgical Materials* is to use the texts with a minimum of prior exposure, letting the texts "introduce themselves," followed by study and reflection. A bibliography on page oo suggests additional education resources for this purpose.

If, on the other hand, this process begins with an introductory educational event, the suggestions above, the bibliographical resources and the questions in the Evaluation (Appendix D, page oo) provide a sense of the direction such a program might take.

Whatever the shape of the process, it is vital that it include children and youth. In fact, the imagination of the child will manifest in the study process and instinctive ease with the range of images at work. This openness is difficult for the adult, whose willingness to 'play' with language has been constrained by experience in life.

Communication and evaluation: The Standing Liturgical Commission, the Church, and Future Prayers

As this book goes to press, the Standing Liturgical Commission is developing a process to guide the use of these *Materials* and to provide for ongoing evaluation. (Some suggestions for beginning an evaluative process in the parish are printed below.) These guidelines will be communicated to the church early in the triennium. The most important aspect of the evaluation of this triennium's work is that the *Materials* continue to provide stimulus for reflection and prayer throughout the church and that suggestions be made about their improvement.

In addition to the evaluation of the *Materials*, the Commission will provide the church with further guidelines for those individuals and congregations who in this process have been inspired to compose their own prayers. The emergence of such new prayers is of great interest to the Commission, as it seeks to encourage a broader participation in the ongoing development of our liturgical life.

The Rev. Sarah Motley

Introduction

Language with Respect to People

One of the results of the increased participation of women in public life has been an increasing dissatisfaction with the historic "masculine-biased" language of public discourse. In recent years it has become common practice to avoid the generic use of the word "men" and, when both sexes are intended, to replace it with "men and women." Similarly, "he or she" and "his or her" now appear in places where our forebears would unhesitatingly have written "he" or "his."

It was during the time that the 1979 Book of Common Prayer was being prepared that the Episcopal Church was confronted with the necessity of taking such changes in the use of language seriously. The result is a Prayer Book which (apart from Rite One services) introduced the practice of using inclusive language when speaking of people.

The translation of the Psalms may serve as an example. Except in passages traditionally understood as messianic (where "man" or "he" is understood by Christians to refer to Jesus), generic uses of nouns and pronouns are avoided. In many instances—where it is clear that both men and women are being referred to—the translation uses the plural: "Blessed are they" rather than "blessed is he," despite the fact that the Hebrew original is in the singular. In other places, "one" or "the one" is used instead of "man" or "he."

Such ways of translating, pioneered in the Prayer Book, can now be seen applied to the whole bible in the *New Revised Standard Version*, published in 1989.

Language with Respect to God

In the Scriptures, God is figured predominantly as male. Such terms as "Father," "Lord," and "King" are obvious examples. Considerable use is also made of "non-gender-specific" names and titles, such as "Rock" (Deuteronomy 32:4), "Redeemer" (Job 19:25), "Savior" (Psalm 88:1) and "Holy One" (Habakkuk 3:3). In a few places, feminine imagery is employed, such as when God is described as a woman in labor (Isaiah 42:14), and as a comforting mother (Isaiah 66:13).

Jesus of Nazareth, as God incarnate, was born and lived as a male human being. He is "Son of God" (Luke 1:35) and "Son of David" (Matthew 9:27). He is also called God's "Word" (John 1:14), God's "wisdom" (1 Corinthians 1:24) and God's "child" or "servant" (Acts 4:27). He is the "Holy One" (Acts 3:14); he is "Lord" (Ephesians 2:11), "Savior" (Titus 1:4), and "Messiah" or "Christ" (John 1:41). Some of these terms are overtly (and appropriately) masculine; others are not. And in one passage, Jesus compares himself to a mother hen anxious to gather her brood under her wings (Matthew 23:37; Luke 13:34-35).

The point to be noted is that ancient Christian prayers made far greater use of this wide range of expression than those composed in later centuries. The eucharistic prayer in the third- century *Apostolic Tradition* of Hippolytus, for example, refers to Jesus as Savior, Redeemer, Messenger, Child, Christ, Word, and Son. Nowhere in the prayer do the words "Lord" or "Father" occur, although Hippolytus uses them in other prayers. What seems to have happened is that with the passage of time a "standard" terminology emerged, in which "Father," "Son," "Christ," and "Lord" were the principal terms employed. Part of the reason for this, no doubt, lies in the commendable efforts of the Church in the fifth century to reinforce Nicene orthodoxy by means of liturgical prayer. That these efforts also resulted in the loss of much rich biblical imagery can, however, reasonably be regretted. The new prayers in this book deliberately seek to recover the use of some long-neglected terms.

A word also needs to be said about pronouns. The increasing disuse of "he," "his," and "him" in a generic sense — that is, to describe both males and females — has had one unexpected result. When used to refer to God, they can seem even more masculine than they did before. In the new prayers in this book, therefore, the use of such pronouns is avoided, except when referring to Jesus.

The Texts in This Book

Specific comment with regard to each text in this book will be found in the Notes that follow each one. Only a few general observations will be made here.

Since the Daily Office consists primarily of biblical texts, the task of providing supplementary materials for those services consisted largely of searching the Scriptures for new texts and of producing new translations of existing material.

In the case of the Eucharist, the task was mainly producing new material, especially eucharistic prayers. In so doing, careful attention was paid to the classic form and content of such prayers.

The core of any Christian eucharistic prayer is the proclamation before God of the Paschal Mystery of Christ—the passion, death, resurrection, and ascension of our Savior. In classical prayers, this core is set in the context of the entire history of salvation, from creation to the consummation of all things. In the course of history, many such prayers have been produced. The reason for the multiplication is not, however, simply a desire for variety, but the fact that no one prayer can possibly say all that deserves to be said.

The four eucharistic prayers provided in the Prayer Book for use in Rite Two illustrate the tradition very well. Each has a characteristic emphasis. Prayer A focuses on the crucifixion, Prayer B on the Incarnation. Prayer C places special emphasis on creation and the fall; while Prayer D., in addition to these themes, dwells on Jesus' life and ministry. The three supplementary prayers in this book follow the same tradition: each has its own special emphasis.

In addition to the three complete eucharistic prayers,[1] this book includes two forms for eucharistic prayer modeled on those on pages 402-405 of the Prayer Book. The primary purpose of such forms is, of course, to make possible the composition of prayers suitable for use by special groups on particular occasions. They may also be used by talented persons to produce prayers of wider interest. It is hoped that composers of such prayers, especially ones which have "worn well" in continued use, will submit them to the commission for possible inclusion in a future book of this kind.

Finally, it should again be noted that this book is a collection of resources. It can, therefore, be used selectively. Some may choose to use much of its contents; others may prefer to be more selective in their choices. It is hoped, however, that all of the material will receive enough use that its value may be thoroughly tested.

In offering this collection to the Church, the commission affirms its belief that the truest test of any liturgical formula is its ability to commend itself to worshippers as a vehicle by which their faith in God can be nourished and strengthened. For that reason, it does not regard this collection as either definitive or final. It is, as stated above, intended as a contribution to an ongoing search — a search that properly belongs to the Church as a whole.

---

[1]The third prayer, based on Wisdom literature, approved by General Convention for continued study and refinement by the Standing Liturgical Commission in consultation with the Theology Committee of the House of Bishops, but not for liturgical use, is not printed in this book. The text can be found on page 268 of the *Blue Book-1991*.

Supplemental Liturgical Materials

Morning and Evening Prayer

Opening Sentences

Advent

Arise, O Jerusalem, stand upon the height and look toward the east, and see your children gathered from west and east at the word of the Holy One. *Baruch 5:5*

Christmas

The Word became flesh and dwelt among us, full of grace and truth. *John 1:14*

Lent

Jesus said: "If any of you would come after me, deny yourself and take up your cross and follow me." *Mark 8:34*

Holy Week

Christ Jesus, being found in human form, humbled himself and became obedient unto death, even death on a cross. *Philippians 2:8*

Occasions of Thanksgiving

We give you thanks, O God, we give you thanks, calling upon your Name and declaring all your wonderful deeds.   *Psalm 75:1*

All Saints and Major Saints' Days

You are no longer strangers and sojourners, but citizens together with the saints and members of the household of God.   *Ephesians 2:19*

At Any Time

God is Spirit, and those who worship must worship in spirit and in truth.   *John 4:24*

NOTES

Advent (Baruch 5:5). A new sentence with an emphasis on the theme of expectation and the eschatological nature of the season, without masculine imagery.

Christmas (John 1:14). A new sentence which incorporates the metaphor of the Word.

Lent (Mark 8:34). A new translation of a Prayer Book text.

Holy Week (Philippians 2:8). A new sentence centered on the sacrifice of the cross.

Occasions of Thanksgiving (Psalm 75:1). An acclamation of praise without gender-related language.

Saints' Days (Ephesians 2:19). A new translation of a Prayer Book text.

At Any Time (John 4:24). A new sentence which identifies God as Spirit.

Absolution

Almighty God have mercy on you, forgive you all your sins through the grace of Jesus Christ, strengthen you in all goodness, and by the power of the Holy Spirit keep you in eternal life. *Amen.*

Opening Versicle

Morning Prayer

Officiant   O God, let our mouth proclaim your praise.
People   *And your glory all the day long.*

Evening Prayer

Officiant   O God, be not far from us.
People   Come quickly to help us, O God.

NOTE

The morning versicle is drawn from Psalm 71:8. In medieval offices it was part of the suffrages at Prime. The evening versicle is from Psalm 71:12.

Doxology

Praise to the holy and undivided Trinity, one God: as it was in the beginning, is now, and will be for ever. Amen.

NOTE

This doxology focuses on the unity of the Triune God. It is similiar to the opening doxology of Byzantine Vespers, which reads, "Glory to the holy, consubstantial, lifegiving and undivided Trinity: always, now and ever, and to ages of ages." The opening words "Praise to" distinguish it from other forms.

Antiphons on Venite or Jubilate

In Advent

Our God and Savior now draws near: O come let us worship.

From the Epiphany through the Baptism of Christ, and on the Feasts of the Transfiguration and Holy Cross

Christ has shown forth his glory: O come let us worship.

In Lent

Our God is full of compassion and mercy: O come let us worship.

or this

Today, if you would hear God's voice: harden not your hearts.

From Easter Day until the Ascension

Alleluia. Christ is risen. O come let us worship. Alleluia.

On Trinity Sunday

The holy and undivided Trinity, one God: O come let us worship.

On other Sundays

Christ has triumphed over death: O come let us worship.

On other Sundays and Weekdays

God is the Rock of our salvation: O come let us worship.

or this

The Holy One is in our midst: O come let us worship.

On All Saints and other Major Saints' Days

The bracketed Alleluia in this Antiphon are used only in Easter Season.

[Alleluia.] Our God is glorious in all the saints: O come let us worship. [Alleluia.]

NOTES

The Latin original of the second half of these antiphons, "Venite adoremus," contains no masculine pronoun. The translation provided is taken from the Canadian *Book of Alternative Services* and retains the number of syllables required for Anglican chant. The *Lutheran Book of Worship* also retains the "O."

Advent. "God" is substituted for "King."

Epiphany. "The Lord" is changed to "Christ" following the precedent of the Latin original.

Lent. "The Lord" is changed to "Our God" as consistent with the psalm passage. An alternative antiphon "Today . . ." derives from the text of Psalm 95. It is an ancient antiphon for Lent.

Trinity Sunday. A new antiphon which is not gender-related. It is similar to the medieval Latin antiphon appointed for this day, which reads, "The true God, One in Trinity and Trinity in Unity, O come let us worship."

Other Sundays. A new antiphon which clearly identifies Sunday as the day of resurrection.

Other Sundays and Weekdays. Two new antiphons which identify God as the Rock of our salvation and as the Holy One.

Saints' Days. "Our God" is substituted for "the Lord," and "the" is substituted for "his."

Morning Psalms

In place of an Invitatory Psalm, one of the following Morning Psalms may be sung or said.

Suggested Antiphons for use with these Psalms will be found on page 23.

Psalm 63:1-8 *Deus, Deus meus*

O God, you are my God; eagerly I seek you;*
    my soul thirsts for you, my flesh faints for you,
        as in a barren and dry land where there is no water.
Therefore I have gazed upon you in your holy place,*
    that I might behold your power and your glory.

For your loving-kindness is better than life itself;*
    my lips shall give you praise.
So will I bless you as long as I live*
    and lift up my hands in your Name.
My soul is content, as with marrow and fatness,*
    and my mouth praises you with joyful lips,
When I remember you upon my bed,*
    and meditate on you in the night watches.
For you have been my helper,*
    and under the shadow of your wings I will rejoice.
My soul clings to you;*
    your right hand holds me fast.

Psalm 67:1-5 *Deus misereatur*

O God, be merciful to us and bless us,*
    show us the light of your countenance and come to us.
Let your ways be known upon earth,*
    your saving health among all nations.
Let the peoples praise you, O God;*
    let all the peoples praise you.
Let the nations be glad and sing for joy,*
    for you judge the peoples with equity
    and guide all the nations upon earth.
Let the peoples praise you, O God;*
    let all the peoples praise you.

NOTES

Psalm 63 is a traditional morning psalm and is used in many ancient forms of the morning office. It also appears as an alternative to Venite or Jubilate in the Canadian *Book of Alternative Services*. It does not refer to God in masculine terms.

Psalm 67 is provided as an alternative to Venite or Jubilate in the new Roman Catholic *Liturgy of the Hours* and in some other modern service books. It does not refer to God in masculine terms and, unlike Psalm 63, is couched in the plural. Following the precedent of *The Psalms: A New Translation* (England, The Grail, 1963), the opening verse is addressed directly to God.

Evening Psalms

In place of or in addition to, Phos hilaron or some other hymn, one of the following Evening Psalms may be sung or said.

Suggested Antiphons for use with these Psalms will be found on page 23.

Psalm 134   *Ecce nunc*

Behold now, bless the LORD, all you servants of the LORD, *
    you that stand by night in the house of the LORD.
Lift up your hands in the holy place and bless the LORD; *
    the LORD who made heaven and earth bless you out of Zion.

Psalm 141:1-3,8ab   *Domine, clamavi*

O LORD, I call to you; come to me quickly; *
    hear my voice when I cry to you.
Let my prayer be set forth in your sight as incense, *
    the lifting up of my hands as the evening sacrifice.
Set a watch before my mouth, O LORD,
and guard the door of my lips; *
    let not my heart incline to any evil thing.
My eyes are turned to you, Lord GOD; *
    in you I take refuge.

NOTES

Psalm 134 is a traditional evening psalm used as in invitatory in the *Alternative Service Book* of the Church of England and in the Canadian *Book of Alternative Services*. While it uses the word "Lord" it contains no masculine overtones.

Psalm 141 is the opening psalm in the oldest known forms of the evening office. It occupies this same position in the *Lutheran Book of Worship* and in a number of other modern service books.

Antiphons for Morning and Evening Psalms

On Psalm 63

O God, you are my God; from break of day I seek you.

On Psalm 67

Let the peoples praise you, O God; let all the peoples praise you.

On Psalm 134

Yours is the day, O God, yours also the night; you established the moon and the sun.

On Psalm 141

Let my prayer be set forth in your sight as incense, the lifting up of my hands as the evening sacrifice.

In the seasons of Advent, Christmas, Lent, and Easter, and on Holy Days, antiphons drawn from the opening sentences given in the Offices, or from other passages of Scripture, my be used instead.

NOTES

Psalm 63. This text is the traditional antiphon, and derives from the Greek version of the first verse of the psalm, which specifically mentions daybreak.

Psalm 67. The antiphon is taken from the psalm itself.

Psalm 134. The text is from Psalm 74:15, which is also appointed as an opening sentence at Evening Prayer (BCP p. 115).

Psalm 141. This text is a traditional antiphon and is drawn from the psalm itself. It is also appointed as an opening sentence at Evening Prayer (BCP p. 115).

The suggestion that the texts of the seasonal opening sentences might be used as antiphons is also derived from the Prayer Book (p. 141).

Canticle 12

A Song of Creation   *Benedicite, omnia opera Domini*
Song of the Three Young Men, 35-65

*One or more sections of this Canticle may be used. Whatever the
selection, it begins with the Invocation and concludes with the Doxology.*

Invocation

Glorify the Lord, all you works of the Lord, *
   sing praise and give honor for ever.
In the high vault of heaven, glorify the Lord, *
   sing praise and give honor for ever.

I. The Cosmic Order

Glorify the Lord, you angels and all powers of the Lord, *
   O heavens and all waters above the heavens.
Sun and moon and stars of the sky, glorify the Lord, *
  sing praise and give honor for ever.

Glorify the Lord, every shower of rain and fall of dew, *
   all winds and fire and heat.
Winter and summer, glorify the Lord, *
   sing praise and give honor for ever.

Glorify the Lord, O chill and cold, *
   drops of dew and flakes of snow.
Frost and cold, ice and sleet, glorify the Lord, *
   sing praise and give honor for ever.

Glorify the Lord, O nights and days, *
   O shining light and enfolding dark.
Storm clouds and thunderbolts, glorify the Lord, *
   sing praise and give honor for ever.

II. The Earth and Its Creatures

Let the earth glorify the Lord, *

sing praise and give honor for ever.
Glorify the Lord, O mountains and hills,
and all that grows upon the earth, *
sing praise and give honor for ever.

Glorify the Lord, O springs of water, seas, and streams, *
O whales and all that move in the waters.
All birds of the air, glorify the Lord, *
sing praise and give honor for ever.

Glorify the Lord, O beasts of the wild, *
and all you flocks and herds.
O men and women everywhere, glorify the Lord, *
sing praise and give honor for ever.

III. *The People of God*

Let the people of God glorify the Lord, *
sing praise and give honor for ever.
Glorify the Lord, O priests and servants of the Lord, *
sing praise and give honor for ever.

Glorify the Lord, O spirits and souls of the righteous, *
sing praise and give honor for ever.
You that are holy and humble of heart, glorify the Lord, *
sing praise and give honor for ever.

Doxology

Let us glorify the Lord: Father, Son and Holy Spirit; *
sing praise and give honor for ever.
In the high vault of heaven, glorify the Lord, *
sing praise and give honor for ever.

NOTE

In this version the refrain has been translated with verbs that do not require an object. "In the high vault of heaven, glorify the Lord" restores the text of the original Latin doxology.

Canticle 15

The Song of Mary   *Magnificat*

A translation recommended by the English Language Liturgical Consultation (ELLC) will be found on page 56.

Canticle 16

The Song of Zechariah   *Benedictus Dominus Deus*

A translation recommended by the English Liturgical Consultation (ELLC) will be found on page 55.

Canticle 18

A Song to the Lamb   *Dignus es*

Revelation 4:11; 5:9-10, 13

Splendor and honor and royal power *
  are yours by right, O God Most High,
For you created everything that is, *
  and by your will they were created and have their being;

And yours by right, O Lamb that was slain, *
  for with your blood you have redeemed for God,
From every family, language, people, and nation, *
  a royal priesthood to serve our God.

And so, to the One who sits upon the throne, *
  and to Christ the Lamb,
Be worship and praise, dominion and splendor, *
  for ever and for evermore.

NOTE.

The Prayer Book translation of this canticle paraphrases the original text; this translation is also paraphrastic and has the advantage of being more inclusive: "Royal power," "O God Most High," "royal priesthood," and "the One."

Canticle 21

We Praise You, O God   *Te Deum laudamus*
The translation recommended by ELLC will be found on page 54.

Additional Canticle A

A Song of Wisdom   *Sapientia liberavit*
Wisdom 10:15-19,20b-21

Wisdom freed from a nation of oppressors *
  a holy people and a blameless race.
She entered the soul of a servant of the Lord, *
  withstood dread rulers with wonders and signs.

To the saints she gave the reward of their labors, *
  and led them by a marvelous way;
She was their shelter by day *
  and a blaze of stars by night.

She brought them across the Red Sea, *
  she led them through mighty waters;
But their enemies she swallowed in the waves *
  and spewed them out from the depths of the abyss.

And then, Lord, the righteous sang hymns to your Name, *
  and praised with one voice your protecting hand;
For Wisdom opened the mouths of the mute, *
  and gave speech to the tongues of a new-born people.

NOTE.

This is a translation from the original Greek of a text which is also found in the Canadian *Book of Alternative Services*. God's salvation is found through Wisdom, who leads her people through the Red Sea and makes for herself a holy people.

Additional Canticle B

A Song of Pilgrimage *Priusquam errarem*
Ecclesiasticus 51:13-16,20b-22

Before I ventured forth,
even while I was very young, *
  I sought wisdom openly in my prayer.
In the forecourts of the temple I asked for her, *
  and I will seek her to the end.
From first blossom to early fruit, *
  she has been the delight of my heart.
My foot has kept firmly to the true path, *
  diligently from my youth have I pursued her.
I inclined my ear a little and received her; *
  I found for myself much wisdom and became adept in her.
To the one who gives me wisdom will I give glory, *
  for I have resolved to live according to her way.
From the beginning I gained courage from her, *
  therefore I will not be foresaken.
In my inmost being I have been stirred to seek her, *
  therefore have I gained a good possession.
As my reward the Almighty has given me the gift of language, *
  and with it will I offer praise to God.

NOTE

This is a canticle from the Mozarabic (medieval Spanish) Psalter, and is a new translation from the Latin. It sees as Wisdom's gift not only the ability to "live according to her way" but also to offer praise and glory to God.

The Apostles' Creed

The translation recommended by ELLC will be found on page 50.

Alternative to the Salutation

Officiant   Hear our cry, O God.
People   And listen to our prayer.
Officiant   Let us pray.

NOTE

The use of a supplicatory verse in place of "The Lord be with you" and its reply was common in medieval forms of the office. See BCP Noonday and Compline for example of this usage. This text is drawn from Psalm 61:1.

Suffrages For Use in Morning Prayer

V.   Help us, O God our Savior;
R.   Deliver us and forgive us our sins.
V.   Look upon your congregation;
R.   Give to your people the blessing of peace
V.   Declare your glory among the nations;
R.   And your wonders among all peoples.
V.   Let not the oppressed by shamed and turned away;
R.   Never forget the lives of your poor.
V.   Continue your loving-kindness to those who know you;
R.   And your favor to those who are true of heart.
V.   Satisfy us by your loving-kindness in the morning;
R.   So shall we rejoice and be glad all the days of our life.

NOTE

This is a new set of suffrages which avoids gender-specific language for God. Source are Psalms 79:9, 74:2, 29:11b, 96:3, 74:20a, 74:18b, 36:10, 90:14.

Concluding Sentence

Glory to God whose power, working in us, can do infinitely more than we can ask or imagine: Glory to God from generation to generation in the Church, and in Christ Jesus for ever and ever. *Amen. Ephesians 3:20,21*

NOTE

"Glory to God" in the second clause provides a more vigorous statement. For precedent in altering concluding sentences for liturgical reasons, see the familiar "Grace;" where the "you" of 2 Corinthians 13:14 has been changed to "us."

Order of Worship for the Evening

Opening Acclamations

From Easter Day through the Day of Pentecost

Officiant   Christ has risen as he promised. Alleluia.
People   And has appeared to the disciples. Alleluia.

or this

Officiant   Stay with us, Christ, for it is evening. Alleluia.
People   Illuminate your Church with your radiance. Alleluia.

In Lent and on other penitential occasions

Officiant   Blessed by the God of our salvation:
People   Who bears our burdens and forgives our sins.

NOTE

The Easter acclamations given here draw on the accounts of Jesus' resurrection appearances but do not use the term "Lord."
For the Lenten acclamation, see page 31.

Evening Psalms

See page 22.

Blessings

See page 49.

The Holy Eucharist

Opening Acclamations

Celebrant   Blessed be the one, holy, and living God.
People   Glory to God for ever and ever.

From Easter Day through the Day of Pentecost

Celebrant   Alleluia. Christ is risen.
People   Christ is risen indeed. Alleluia.

In Lent and on other penitential occasions

Celebrant   Blessed be the God of our salvation:
People   Who bears our burdens and forgives our sins.

NOTES

The practice of beginning the eucharistic celebration with an acclamation is Byzantine in origin, and was first introduced into Anglican liturgy in the 1979 Prayer Book.

The first of those provided here acclaims God in terms common to both Jewish and Christian belief. See Deuteronomy 6:4, Leviticus 19:2, Psalm 42:2, Mark 12:32, Revelation 4:8, John 6:57.

The second is a revision of the Prayer Book acclamation for Easter Season.

The Lenten acclamation is based on Psalms 68:19 and 103:3.

Song of Praise

The rubics of the Prayer Book (p. 356) provide that "some other song of praise" may be used in place of the Gloria in excelsis. Canticle 18, A Song to the Lamb, is recommended. See page 26. Like the Gloria in excelsis, this canticle is a hymn to God and to the Lamb.

Salutation

Celebrant	May God be with you.
People	And also with you.

NOTE

Historic liturgies show some variety in the wording of the salutation.
A simple alternative is provided here.

Gospel Announcement

The Holy Gospel of our Savior Jesus Christ according to _____.

NOTE

This form places the emphasis on Jesus as "Savior." The term "Lord" is emphasized in the people's response.

The Nicene Creed

The translation recommended by the English Language Liturgical Consultation [ELLC] will be found on page 51.

Prayers of the People

This book contains no forms for the Prayers of the People. Rather, it calls attention to the generous and flexible — and frequently overlooked — provisions of the Book of Common Prayer.

Of the six forms provided (BCP pp. 383-393), none are required. Any of them *may* be used or adapted to the occasion. They may also be replaced by other forms. All that is required is that the topics listed at the top of page 383 be included in the prayers.

The six forms provided may also be used as models for the creation of new forms. A few suggestions follow.

Form II has its roots in the practice of the Church in the earliest centuries. It consists simply of a series of biddings, covering the required topics (to which others may be added), each followed by silence. The intent is that the silences be long enough that the congregation is given opportunity for serious silent intercession.

Forms I and V follow the pattern of classical litanies, and are in each case addressed to the Second Person of the Trinity.

Form I is the simpler of the two, and consists of a series of biddings addressed to the congregation, most of them introduced by the word "for" and concluded by a congregational petition addressed to Christ. A form based on this model might begin:

In peace and in faith, let us offer our prayers, saying, "Christ, have mercy."

For peace and tranquility in the world, and for the salvation of all, let us pray.

Christ, have mercy.

For N. our Presiding Bishop, for N.(N.) our own Bishop(s), and for all the People of God, let us pray.

Christ, have mercy.

For V consists of a series of petitions addressed directly to Christ, each beginning with "for," but frequently including a result clause beginning with "that." A form based on this model might begin:

We pray to you, O Christ Our God, saying, "Christ, have mercy" (or "Christe eleison").

For the Church of God in every place, that it may persevere in faith and hope, we pray to you.

Christ, have mercy. (Christe eleison.)

For all who minister in your Church, (especially _____,) that they may have grace to build up your people in love, we pray to you.

Christ, have mercy. (Christe eleison.)

Form IV consists of a series of petitions addressed to the First Person of the Trinity, each followed by an invariable versicle and response which is easily memorized. The following might be used:

God of love and mercy,
Hear our prayer.

Forms III and VI are examples of responsive prayer. Unlike the other forms, they require that the complete text be available to all the worshipers. Form VI, when used as a model, also provides an opportunity to compose and use other forms for the Confession of Sin.

The rubrics (BCP p. 394) do not require that the Collect that concludes the Prayers be drawn from the Prayer Book. Celebrants and others involved in the planning of liturgy are therefore free to compose new Collects, both for the general use and for the seasons and holy days of the Church Year.

Absolution

See above under Morning and Evening Prayer on page 17.

The Peace

Celebrant	The peace of Christ be always with you.
People	And also with you.

Eucharistic Prayer 1

Celebrant	The Lord be with you.
People	And also with you.
Celebrant	Lift up your hearts.
People	We lift them to the Lord.
Celebrant	Let us give thanks to the Lord our God.
People	It is right to give God thanks and praise.

Celebrant   It is truly right, and good and joyful,
to give you thanks, all-holy God,
source of life and fountain of mercy.

The following Preface may be used at any time.

You have filled us and all creation with your blessing
and fed us with your constant love;
you have redeemed us in Jesus Christ
and knit us into one body.
Through your Spirit you replenish us
and call us to fullness of life.

In place of the preceding, a Proper Preface from the Book of Common Prayer may be used.

Therefore, joining with Angels and Archangels
and with the faithful of every generation,
we lift our voices with all creation as we sing (say):

Celebrant and People

Holy, holy, holy Lord, God of power and might,
heaven and earth are full of your glory.

Hosanna in the highest.
Blessed is the one who comes in the name of the Lord.
Hosanna in the highest.

The Celebrant continues

Blessed are you, gracious God,
creator of the universe and giver of life.
You formed us in your own image
and called us to dwell in your infinite love.
You gave the world into our care
that we might be your faithful stewards
and show forth your bountiful grace.

But we failed to honor your image
in one another and in ourselves;
we would not see your goodness in the world around us;
and so we violated your creation,
abused one another,
and rejected your love.
Yet you never creased to care for us,
and prepared the way of salvation for all people.

Through Abraham and Sarah
you called us into covenant with you.
You delivered us from slavery,
sustained us in the wilderness,
and raised up prophets
to renew your promise of salvation.
Then, in the fullness of time,
you sent your eternal Word,
made mortal flesh in Jesus.
Born into the human family,
and dwelling among us,
he revealed our glory.
Giving himself freely to death on the cross,
he triumphed over evil,
opening the way of freedom and life.

36

At the following words concerning the bread, the Celebrant is to hold it, or lay a hand upon it; and at the words concerning the cup, to hold or place a hand upon the cup and any other vessel containing wine to be consecrated.

On the night before he died for us,
Our Savior Jesus Christ took bread,
and when he had given thanks to you,
he broke it, and gave it to his friends, and said:
"Take, eat:
This is my Body which is given for you.
Do this for the remembrance of me."
As supper was ending, Jesus took the cup of wine,
and when he had given thanks,
he gave it to them, and said:
"Drink this, all of you:
This is my Blood of the new Covenant,
which is poured out for you and for all
for the forgiveness of sins.
Whenever you drink it,
do this for the remembrance of me."

Therefore we proclaim the mystery of faith:

Celebrant and People

Christ has died.
Christ is risen.
Christ will come again.

The Celebrant continues

Remembering his death and resurrection,
we now present to you from your creation
this bread and this wine.
By your Holy Spirit may they be for us
the Body and Blood of our Savior Jesus Christ.
Grant that we who share these gifts
may be filled with the Holy Spirit
and live as Christ's Body in the world.

Bring us into the everlasting heritage
of your daughters and sons,
that with [_____ and] all your saints,
past, present, and yet to come,
we may praise your Name for ever.

Through Christ and with Christ and in Christ,
in the unity of the Holy Spirit,
to you be honor, glory, and praise,
for ever and ever. *AMEN.*

NOTES

For comment on the opening dialogue and on the Sanctus, see page 53.

The Preface of this prayer, which may be used at any time, has as its theme the abundance of God's love for us. A rubric provides that a Proper Preface from the Book of Common Prayer may be used instead, thus making it possible to introduce a commemoration of the liturgical season or occasion.

The paragraph leading into the Sanctus reminds us that we join, not only with the heavenly chorus of angels, but with the faithful of every generation and with all creation in giving praise to God.

In the post-Sanctus portion of the thanksgiving, the prayer blesses God who is the source of life. We who are made in the image of God acknowledge the responsibility of being made stewards of God's creation (Genesis 1:26-28). We also acknowledge our sinfulness, and its effects on ourselves, on others, and on the creation itself.

God's faithfulness, despite our sin, is recalled in the history of salvation. We remember the convenant relationship between God and the people of God "through Abraham and Sarah" (Genesis 17:1,15-19), the deliverance of Israel from slavery and their sustenance in the wilderness (Exodus), and the proclamation of the prophets (see also Luke 1:68-79). The Incarnation is part of this salvation history, occurring in the fullness of time. It is described in Johannine terms as the Word becoming flesh and revealing God's grace and glory (John 1:14).

In the institution narrative, the word "friends" is used in place of "disciples." This same usage can be seen in the Prayer Book in Eucharistic Prayer C (p. 371) and in Form 1 on page 403. The source of the term is John 15:13-15, where Jesus at the Last Supper says, "I do not call you servants any longer . . .
I have called you friends."

38

In the paragraph concerning the cup, the narrative begins with the words, "As supper was ending . . ." This wording recognizes that the sharing of a last cup at a Jewish formal meal is not an after-dinner action, but the closing ritual of the meal itself.

The narrative goes on to speak of the Blood of the New Covenant "poured out for you and for all." "Poured out" is the translation used in the *Revised Standard Version* of the Bible (Matthew 26:28, Mark 13:24), and is chosen here to emphasize the double level of significance: blood is "poured out" from a wound, and wine is also "poured out." The use of "all" makes it clear that forgiveness of sins is made available to all through Christ's sacrifice. While the Greek word is literally translated "many," biblical scholars have pointed out that in the context of the passage it means that the sacrifice is made not just for a large number of persons, but for all humanity. (A similar use of "many" occurs in Matthew 20:28, where it is written that Jesus would give his life as a ransom for many." First Timothy 2:6, looking back on the event, says he gave himself as a "ransom for all.") New eucharistic prayers in both the Roman Catholic Church and the Lutheran Church use "all" rather than "many."

The memorial acclamation is familiar from Eucharistic Prayer A and is chosen to provide an easily remembered response by the people. After remembering Jesus' death and resurrection, and offering the gifts of bread and wine, the prayer invokes the Holy Spirit upon the bread and wine and upon the people. We ask that we might live as Christ's Body in the world, a reminder that we are already the Body of Christ by virtue of our baptism and need God's grace to live out our baptismal covenant. Finally, we pray that we might join with all God's saints, past, present, and yet to come, in everlasting praise of God.

Eucharistic Prayer 2

Celebrant	The Lord be with you.
People	And also with you.
Celebrant	Lift up your hearts.
People	We lift them to the Lord.
Celebrant	Let us give thanks to the Lord our God.
People	It is right to give God thanks and praise.

Celebrant

We praise you and we bless you, holy and gracious God,
source of life abundant.
From before time you made ready the creation.

Your Spirit moved over the deep
and brought all things into being:
sun, moon, and stars;
earth, winds, and waters;
and every living thing.
You made us in your image, male and female,
and taught us to walk in your ways.
But we rebelled against you, and wandered far away;
and yet, as a mother cares for her children,
you would not forget us.
Time and again you called us
to live in the fullness of your love.

And so this day we join with Saints and Angels
in the chorus of praise that rings through eternity,
lifting our voices to magnify you as we sing (say):

Celebrant and People

Holy, holy, holy Lord, God of power and might,
heaven and earth are full of your glory.
   Hosanna in the highest.
Blessed is the one who comes in the name of the Lord.
   Hosanna in the highest.

The Celebrant continues

Glory and honor and praise to you, holy and living God.
To deliver us from the power of sin and death
and to reveal the riches of your grace,
you looked with favor upon Mary, your willing servant,
that she might conceive and bear a son,
Jesus the holy child of God.
Living among us, Jesus loved us.
He broke bread with outcasts and sinners,
healed the sick, and proclaimed good news to the poor.
He yearned to draw all the world to himself
yet we were heedless of his call to walk in love.
Then, the time came for him to complete upon the cross

the sacrifice of his life,
and to be glorified by you.

*At the following words concerning the bread, the Celebrant is to hold it,
or lay a hand upon it; and at the words concerning the cup, to hold or
place a hand upon the cup and any other vessel containing the wine to be
consecrated.*

On the night before he died for us,
Jesus was at table with his friends.
He took bread, gave thanks to you,
broke it, and gave it to them, and said:
"Take, eat:
This is my Body, which is given for you.
Do this for the remembrance of me."
As supper was ending, Jesus took the cup of wine.
Again, he gave thanks to you,
gave it to them, and said:
"Drink this, all of you:
This is my Blood of the new Covenant,
which is poured out for you and for all
for the forgiveness of sins.
Whenever you drink it,
do this for the remembrance of me."

Now gathered at your table, O God of all creation,
and remembering Christ, crucified and risen,
who was and is and is to come,
we offer to you our gifts of bread and wine,
and ourselves, a living sacrifice.

Pour out your Spirit upon these gifts
that they may be the Body and Blood of Christ.
Breathe your Spirit over the whole earth
and make us your new creation,
the Body of Christ given for the world you have made.

In the fullness of time bring us,
with [N. _____ and] all your saints,

from every tribe and language and people and nation,
to feast at the banquet prepared
from the foundation of the world.

Through Christ and with Christ and in Christ,
in the unity of the Holy Spirit,
to you be honor, glory, and praise,
for ever and ever. *AMEN.*

NOTES

For comments on the opening dialogue and on the Sanctus, see page 53.

The fixed Preface of this prayer begins with an extended thanksgiving for the work of God in creation, based on Genesis 1. This way of beginning is characteristic of many ancient eucharistic prayers, and can be seen in the Prayer Book in Eucharistic Prayer C (p. 370) and in Forms 1 and 2 on pages 402-405. The prayer then goes on to speak briefly of the fall in terms reminiscent of the stories of Adam and Eve and the sin of Cain (Genesis 2:1 — 4:16). The image of God caring for us "as a mother cares for her children" is drawn from Isaiah 49:15-16.

The post-Sanctus portion of the prayer gives thanks for Christ's Incarnation and life among us. "Looked with favor" is a quotation from the cantile Magnificat; "your willing servant" recalls the importance of Mary's assent as told in Luke 1:38. The paragraph continues with references to Jesus' ministry in language drawn from Isaiah 61:1-2, Luke 4:16-21, Matthew 23:37, John 12:32, and Ephesians 5:2.

For comment on the institution narrative, see the Notes on page 38.

Following the narrative, God is again addressed as Creator and Christ proclaimed as crucified and risen. The line "who was and is to come" is from Revelation 4:8. "Ourselves, a living sacrifice" is based on Romans 12:1, and echoes the "reasonable, holy, and living sacrifice unto thee" of Eucharistic Prayer I (BCP p. 336).

"Pour our your Spirit" and "Breathe your Spirit" are expressions drawn from Joel 2:28 and Genesis 2:7, respectively. "New creation" is drawn from 2 Corinthians 5:17.

The line in the last petition, "from every tribe and language and people and nation," is a direct quotation from Revelation 5:9. The imagery of the banquet "prepared from the foundation of the world" is drawn from Matthew 22:1-14, Luke 14:16-24, and Matthew 25:34. See also the Catechism (BCP pp. 859-860), where the Eucharist is described as the "foretaste of the heavenly banquet."

Forms for the Eucharistic Prayer

For use with the Order for Celebrating the Holy Eucharist on pages 400-401 of the Book of Common Prayer. In keeping with the rubrics governing the use of the Order, these forms are not intended for use at the principal Sunday or weekly celebration of a congregation.

FORM A

Celebrant The Lord be with you.
People   And also with you.
Celebrant Lift up your hearts.
People   We lift them to the Lord
Celebrant Let us give thanks to the Lord our God.
People   It is right to give God thanks and praise.

The Celebrant gives thanks to God for the created order, and for God's self-revelation to the human race in history;

Recalls before God, when appropriate, the particular occasion being celebrated;

If desired, incorporates or adapts the Proper Preface of the Day.

> *If the Sanctus is to be included, it is introduced with these or similar words*
> And so we join the saints and angels in proclaiming your glory, as we sing (say),
>
> *Celebrant and People*
>
> Holy, holy, holy Lord, God of power and might,
> heaven and earth are full of your glory.
>   Hosanna in the highest.
> Blessed is the one who comes in the name of the Lord.
>   Hosanna in the highest.

The Celebrant now praises God for the salvation of the world through Christ Jesus.

The Prayer continues with these words

And so, we offer you these gifts.

43

Sanctify them by your Holy Spirit
to be for your people the Body and Blood of Christ.

*At the following words concerning the bread, the Celebrant is to hold it,
or lay a hand upon it; and at the words concerning the cup, to hold or
place a hand upon the cup and any other vessel containing wine to be
consecrated.*

On the night before he died for us,
our Savior Jesus Christ took bread,
and when he had given thanks to you,
he broke it, and gave it to his friends, and said:
"Take, eat:
This is my Body which is given for you.
Do this for the remembrance of me."

As supper was ending, Jesus took the cup of wine,
and when he had given thanks,
he gave it to them, and said:
"Drink this, all of you:
This is my blood of the new Covenant,
which is poured out for you and for all
for the forgiveness of sins.
Whenever you drink it,
do this for the remembrance of me."

*The Celebrant may then introduce, with suitable words, a memorial
acclamation by the people.*

The Celebrant then continues

We now celebrate, O God, the memorial of Christ our Savior.
By means of this holy bread and cup,
we show forth the sacrifice of Christ's death,
and proclaim the resurrection,
until Christ comes in glory.

Gather us by this Holy Communion
into one body in the Risen One,
and make us a living sacrifice of praise.

Through Christ and with Christ and in Christ,
in the unity of the Holy Spirit,
to you be honor, glory, and praise,
for ever and ever. *AMEN.*

FORM B

Celebrant The Lord be with you.
People And also with you.
Celebrant Lift up your hearts.
People We lift them to the Lord.
Celebrant Let us give thanks to the Lord our God.
People It is right to give God thanks and praise.

The Celebrant gives thanks to God for the created order, and for God's self-revelation to the human race in history:

Recalls before God, when appropriate, the particular occasion being celebrated;

If desired, incorporates or adapts the Proper Preface of the Day.

> *If the Sanctus is to be included, it is introduced with these or similar words*
>
> And so we join the saints and angels in proclaiming your glory, as we sing (say),
>
> *Celebrant and People*
>
> Holy, holy, holy Lord, God of power and might,
> heaven and earth are full of your glory.
> Hosanna in the highest.
> Blessed is the one who comes in the name of the Lord.
> Hosanna in the highest.

The Celebrant now praises God for the salvation of the world through Christ Jesus.

At the following words concerning the bread, the Celebrant is to hold it, or lay a hand upon it; and at the words concerning the cup, to hold or place a hand upon the cup and any other vessel containing wine to be consecrated.

45

On the night before he died for us,
our Savior Jesus Christ took bread,
and when he had given thanks to you,
he broke it, and gave it to his friends, and said:
"Take, eat:
This is my Body which is given for you.
Do this for the remembrance of me."

As supper was ending, Jesus took the cup of wine,
and when he had given thanks,
he gave it to them, and said:
"Drink this, all of you:
This is my blood of the new Covenant,
which is poured out for you and for all
for the forgiveness of sins.
Whenever you drink it,
do this for the remembrance of me."

The Celebrant may then introduce, with suitable words, a memorial acclamation by the people.

The Celebrant then continues

Remembering now the suffering and death
and proclaiming the resurrection and ascension
of Jesus our Redeemer,
we bring before you these gifts.
Sanctify them by your Holy Spirit
to be for your people the Body and Blood of Christ.

The Celebrant then prays that all may receive the benefits of Christ's work, and the renewal of the Holy Spirit.

The Prayer concludes with these or similar words

Through Christ and with Christ and in Christ,
in the unity of the Holy Spirit,
to you be honor, glory, and praise,
for ever and ever. *AMEN.*

NOTES

These forms are modeled on Forms 1 and 2 on pages 402-405 of the Book of
Common Prayer. Following the Prayer Book, Form 1 places the invocation of the
Holy Spirit before the words of institution, and Form 2 places it after them.

The texts of the opening dialogue, Sanctus, and concluding doxology are
identical with those in two complete eucharistic prayers (see pages 35 to 42). The
institution narrative is the same as in Eucharistic Prayer 1.

Memorial Acclamation A

Celebrant

In obedience to this command:

Celebrant and People

We remember his death on the cross.
We proclaim the resurrection to new life.
We await Christ's coming in glory.

NOTE

By using the article "the" before the word "resurrection," this acclamation
affirms not only the resurrection of Christ, but also that of all of us who were
"buried with him" in baptism and raised to "newness of life" (Rom. 6:4).

Memorial Acclamation B

Celebrant

In faith we acclaim you, O Christ:

Celebrant and People

Dying, you destroyed our death.
Rising, you restored our life.
Christ Jesus, come in glory.

Fraction Anthems

We break this bread
to share in the Body of Christ.
We who are many are one body,
for we all share in the one bread.

God of promise, you have prepared a banquet for us.
Happy are those who are called to the Supper of the Lamb.

This is the true bread which comes down from heaven and gives
life to the world.
Whoever eats this bread will live for ever.

Lamb of God, you take away the sins of the world:
    have mercy on us.
Lamb of God, you take away the sins of the world:
    have mercy on us.
Lamb of God, you take away the sins of the world:
    grant us peace.

NOTES

The first anthem is based on 1 Corinthians 10:16-17. It is also used at the
breaking of the bread in the *Alternative Services Book* of the Church of England.

The second anthem refers to Communion as a banquet, in words reminiscent
of the Exhortation to Communion (BCP p. 317). The second line is drawn from
Revelation 19:9.

The third anthem is based on John 6:33,50-51.

The fourth anthem is taken from the Book of Common Prayer (p. 407).
Because it is printed under "Additional Directions," rather than in the text of Rite
II, it is frequently overlooked as an option. *The Hymnal 1982* includes four
settings of this anthem.

Postcommunion Prayer

Gracious and loving God,
you have made us one in the body of Christ,
and nourished us at your table
with holy food and drink.
Now send us forth
to be your people in the world.
Grant us strength to persevere in resisting evil,
and to proclaim in all we say and do
your Good News in Christ Jesus our Savior. Amen.

NOTE

The petitions in this prayer are drawn from the Baptismal Covenant on pages
304-305 of the Prayer Book.

Blessings

The blessing of the eternal Majesty,
the incarnate Word,
and the abiding Spirit,
be with you now and for evermore. *Amen.*

Holy eternal Majesty,
Holy incarnate Word,
Holy abiding Spirit,
Bless you for evermore. *Amen.*

May the blessing of the God of Abraham and Sarah, and of Jesus
Christ born of our sister Mary, and of the Holy Spirit, who broods
over the world as a mother over her children, be upon you and
remain with you always. *Amen.*

ELLC Texts

The texts which follow were not prepared by the Episcopal Church. They
are the work of the ecumenical English Language Liturgical Consultation
(ELLC), which has "recommended" them to the churches.

Formed in 1985, the Consultation consists of representatives of the
major English-speaking churches throughout the world, including the
Episcopal and other Anglican churches. Its initial task was to review the
work of its predecessor, the International Consultation on English Texts
(ICET), in the light of "growing indications that these texts are in need of
some revision." The ICET texts themselves were set forth in final form in
1975 in a booklet entitled *Prayers We Have in Common*. Most of these
texts were subsequently incorporated into the 1979 Prayer Book.

It should be noted that, in some instances, the Standing Liturgical
Commission of the Episcopal Church has not accepted the ELLC
recommendations. Where this is the case, the text as printed includes the
commission's revisions, and the reasons for them are discussed in the
Notes that follow.

The Apostles' Creed

I believe in God, the Father almighty,
   creator of heaven and earth.
I believe in Jesus Christ, God's only Son, our Lord,
   who was conceived by the Holy Spirit,
   born of the Virgin Mary,
   suffered under Pontius Pilate,
   was crucified, died, and was buried;
   he descended to the dead.
   On the third day he rose again;

he ascended into heaven,
he is seated at the right hand of the Father,
and he will come again to judge the living and the dead.
I believe in the Holy Spirit,
the holy catholic Church,
the communion of saints,
the forgiveness of sins,
the resurrection of the body,
and the life everlasting. Amen.

NOTE

Except for the substitution of "God's" for "his" in line 3, this is a
straightforward rendition of the Latin text. Note that it does not speak of Jesus'
being conceived by "the power of" the Holy Spirit, since those words do not
occur in the Latin original.

The Nicene Creed

We believe in one God,
the Father, the Almighty,
maker of heaven and earth,
of all that is, seen and unseen.
We believe in one Lord, Jesus Christ,
the only Son of God,
eternally begotten of the Father,
God from God, Light from Light,
true God from true God,
begotten, not made,
of one Being with the Father;
through him all things were made.
For us and for our salvation
he came down from heaven,

was incarnate of the Holy Spirit and the Virgin Mary
and became truly human.
For our sake he was crucified under Pontius Pilate;
he suffered death and was buried.
On the third day he rose again
in accordance with the Scriptures;
he ascended into heaven
and is seated at the right hand of the Father.
He will come again in glory to judge the living and the dead,
and his kingdom will have no end.
We believe in the Holy Spirit, the Lord, the giver of life,
who proceeds from the Father [and the Son],
who with the Father and the Son is worshiped and glorified,
who has spoken through the prophets.
We believe in one holy catholic and apostolic Church.
We acknowledge one baptism for the forgiveness of sins.
We look for the resurrection of the dead,
and the life of the world to come. Amen.

NOTES

This version follows the Greek original precisely in translating line 15 as "was incarnate of the Holy Spirit and the Virgin Mary," thus emphasizing that Mary was an active, rather than a passive, participant in the Incarnation (Luke 1:38). Some early Latin manuscripts agree with this and read "et Maria Virgine." The version that prevailed, however, changed the "et" to "ex."

This version also follows the Greek and Latin (and the English of Rite One) in using "who" rather than "he" in the section about the Holy Spirit.

The words in brackets, "and the Son," are not a part of the original Greek text. They were added to some Latin translations. Since the decision to exclude or include them rests with the particular churches involved in the Consultation, ELLC takes no position on the subject. The Episcopal Church, however, at the General Convention of 1988, placed itself on record as favoring their omission, a decision later approved by the Lambeth Conference.

Sursum Corda

Celebrant The Lord be with you.
People　　And also with you.
Celebrant Lift up your hearts.
People　　We lift them to the Lord.
Celebrant Let us give thanks to the Lord our God.
People　　It is right to give God thanks and praise.

NOTE

The ELLC version of the last line reads "It is right to give our thanks and praise," which is derived from the Canadian *Book of Alternative Services*. The commission's preference is to call attention to God, the object of the thanksgiving, rather than to the worshipers, at this point.

Sanctus

Holy, holy, holy, God of power and might,
heaven and earth are full of your glory.
　Hosanna in the highest.
Blessed is the one who comes in the name of the Lord.
　Hosanna in the highest.

NOTE

The ELLC version of this text reads "Blessed is he" in the fourth line. The text as printed follows the *New Revised Standard Version* of the Bible in translating Matthew 21:9 and Psalm 118:26 as "Blessed is the one . . ."

Te Deum Laudamus

We praise you, O God,
we acclaim you as Lord;
all creation worships you,
the Father everlasting.
To you all angels, all the powers of heaven,
the cherubim and seraphim, sing in endless praise:
    Holy, holy, holy Lord, God of power and might,
    heaven and earth are full of your glory.
The glorious company of apostles praise you.
The noble fellowship of prophets praise you.
The white-robed army of martyrs praise you.
Throughout the world the holy Church acclaims you:
    Father, of majesty unbounded,
    your true and only son, worthy of all worship,
    and the Holy Spirit, advocate and guide.
You, Christ, are the king of glory,
the eternal Son of the Father.
When you took our flesh to set us free
you humbly chose the Virgin's womb.
You overcame the sting of death
and opened the kingdom of heaven to all believers.
You are seated at God's right hand in glory.
We believe that you will come to be our judge.
    Come then, Lord, and help your people,
    bought with the price of your own blood,
    and bring us with your saints
    to glory everlasting.

NOTE

The principal change is in the first line, which is now identical with our
familiar Rite One version. Lines 18 and 19 are also newly translated.

The Song of Zechariah

Blessed are you, Lord, the God of Israel, *
  you have come to your people and set them free.
You have raised up for us a mighty Savior, *
  born of the house of your servant David.
Through your holy prophets you promised of old
to save us from our enemies, *
  from the hands of all who hate us,
To show mercy to our forebears, *
  and to remember your holy covenant.
This was the oath you swore to our father Abraham, *
  to set us free from the hands of our enemies,
Free to worship you without fear, *
  holy and righteous before you,
  all the days of our life.
And you, child, shall be called the prophet
   of the Most High, *
  for you will go before the Lord to prepare the way,
To give God's people knowledge of salvation *
  by the forgiveness of their sins.
In the tender compassion of our God *
  the dawn from on high shall break upon us,
To shine on those who dwell in darkness
   and the shadow of death, *
  and to guide our feet into the way of peace.

NOTE

This translation addresses God in the second, rather than the third, person. As precedent for such a change, see the Sanctus. The text in Isaiah 6 reads "full of *his* glory." For liturgical use, the "his" had been changed to "your."

The Song of Mary

My soul proclaims the greatness of the Lord,
my spirit rejoices in you, O God my Savior, *
   for you have looked with favor on your lowly servant.
From this day all generations will call me blessed: *
   you, the Almighty, have done great things for me,
   and holy is your name.
You have mercy on those who fear you *
   from generation to generation.
You have shown strength with your arm *
   and scattered the proud in their conceit,
Casting down the mighty from their thrones *
   and lifting up the lowly.
You have filled the hungry with good things *
   and sent the rich away empty.
You have come to the help of your servant Israel, *
   for you have remembered your promise of mercy,
The promise made to our forebears, *
   to Abraham and his children for ever.

NOTES

Like the Benedictus, this version is cast in direct address to God, See the note on page 55.

Two changes have been made in the translation recommended by ELLC. The first is in lines 2 and 3, where the ELLC text reads "my spirit rejoices in God my Savior, for you, Lord, have looked with favor . . ." It seemed to the commission more felicitous to establish the fact of direct address in the second line.

The other is in lines 15 and 16, where the ELLC version reads ". . . to the aid of your servant Israel, to remember the promise of mercy," The commission preferred "help" to "aid," and found line 16 awkward.

Background

Leonel L. Mitchell

"The world to which we are sent to proclaim Christ is constantly changing, and the gospel needs to be translated into terms which the world can understand. This means more than translating the actual language of the proclamation . . . It means translating its thought into forms which our culture can comprehend, so that the original message shines through undistorted."[1]

When I wrote these words in 1975, the topic under discussion was the services then undergoing trial use which became the Book of Common Prayer 1979. The situation today is no different. Change is still the only constant factor in our history. At the present moment our concern is ongoing change in the English language and its effect on the way we pray.

Language and Change

Anglicanism for over four centuries has been concerned that people pray in their own language. In the 1970s the Episcopal Church, like most English-speaking churches throughout the world, began to celebrate the liturgy in 20th century English. For 400 years the language of Cranmer and the King James Bible had been determinative for the way in which English-speaking people had framed their prayers. This is no longer true. All across the ecclesiastical spectrum God is regularly addressed in both public and private prayer in contemporary language. Liturgies, whether Anglican, Roman, Lutheran, or Reformed, use formal contemporary speech, and when the Scripture is read, even the Revised Standard Version may sound quaint or antiquated.

One of the characteristics of a living language is that it grows and changes, adding new words to its vocabulary and changing the meanings of existing ones. Words such as "quick" meaning "living" or "prevent" meaning "precede" can no longer be used without their probably being misunderstood. Sometimes words do not change their actual denotation, but gain or lose social acceptability, or positive or negative connotations. They are still understood, but the message they send is distorted. An example of this is the word "stink," which is now always unpleasant and impolite, but which originally referred to any kind of odor.

Changes that have already taken place are one thing, but while change is actually happening, it is more difficult to appreciate and may actually become a source of misunderstanding or heated controversy. Proper names such as the National Association for the Advancement of Colored People and the United Negro College Fund bear witness to the changing ways in which African Americans in this century have referred to themselves. Praying in contemporary English, then, may involve us in a continuous updating of our language, not so that we may say new and different things, but so we may continue to say the same thing without our words distorting what we say.

Technical Language and Liturgical Language

Academic theology, by contrast, has generally operated by carefully defining technical terms to insure precision of meaning. All technical disciplines, including nuclear physics, computer programming, and football coaching, tend to operate this way. The words "strike" and "hit," which are synonyms in ordinary English, mean quite different things to a baseball fan. In academic writing, technical terms are frequently imported from another language to avoid being subject to the varieties of meaning on which the living language thrives. We speak of *ecclesia* to escape the ambiguity of "church," or *anamnesis* to avoid "remembrance" or "memorial," and the eucharistic controversies of the sixteenth century which involved those concepts. Scholars may use this language in their private prayers, but the liturgy must speak a language more accessible to all. This language often lacks the precision of technical theological jargon, and, like all natural language, is capable of many levels of understanding and meaning. It may be poetic and imaginative, but it must speak the truth.

Liturgical language is theological language, but it is not the language of academic theology. It is the language of "primary theology," of address to God. It embodies the images and metaphors in which we think of and speak to our God. This language of prayer and hymn shapes our theological understanding much more surely than articles in theological journals. Anglican theology itself, as much as Anglican piety, has been shaped in this way over the years by the liturgy of the Book of Common Prayer.

Whether in prayer or in academic theology, the language in which we speak of God is necessarily metaphorical, or analogical. We cannot use human words to speak of God in the same sense in which we use them to speak of human beings. Even words like "good" and "powerful" mean something different when applied to God. The words are perhaps the best analogies we can find to the divine attributes, but they are not exact fits.

> For my thoughts are not your thoughts,
> nor your ways my ways, says the Lord.
> For as the heavens are higher than the earth,
> so are my ways higher than your ways,
> and my thoughts than your thoughts.[2]

Any image of God or theological construct we may have is too small, too narrow, and grossly inadequate. Some are more obviously inadequate than others, but when human reason and language have gone as far as they can, there is still further to go and more to comprehend. The Cappadocian Fathers understood this. The great scholastics of the Middle Ages understood this. The Reformers understood it. So did the Caroline divines, and so do contemporary theologians.

Analogous and Literal Language

It is almost impossible for human beings to avoid using anthropomorphic terms in thinking about God, and, even if we are able to avoid such terms in theological discourse, we do not pray to a "prime mover unmoved" or a "first caused uncaused." The more "real" and "personal" our notion of God is, the more anthropomorphic our language is likely to be. As Christian we properly justify the use of such language in terms of the incarnation and the *imago Dei*. Christ is "the image of the invisible God,"[3] and we are all, male and female, made in the divine image.[4]

The great problem of all the figures, images, and metaphors used in the liturgy is that we begin to forget that they are used analogically, an to think of them as literal descriptions. We think of God as wearing a crown, or carrying a shepherd's crook, or seated on a throne. These mental pictures may be devotionally helpful to us, as long as we remember that they are *our* images, not pictures of God in the reality and fullness of the divine being. The more apt the metaphor, the more likely we are to forget that it is a metaphor. When Jesus says, "I am the vine," we all recognize that it is a figure of speech, but we are apt to forget that "I and the Father are one" is not literal description.

Many of the images of God we use in our worship are biblical. Others have their roots in the theological tradition of the early Church. Some are medieval or modern. All are rooted in human understanding and tend to lose or change their meaning as the cultural matrices in which they are grounded change. Marianne Micks wrote, "Symbols slip. All symbols slip. The symbol breakers who have appeared regularly in the Christian community, smashing other men's efforts to figure forth the One whom they worship, have recognized this."[5] Throughout the centuries liturgies have been subject to this slippage.

In the 16th century a favorite metaphor for God was King. In 1547, the year of Henry VIII's death, a prayer still in the English Prayer Book addressed God as "high and mighty, King of Kings, Lord of Lords, the only ruler of Princes, who dost from thy throne behold all the dwellers upon earth."[6] In Tudor England this image of God as a monarch on a lofty throne with faithful subjects humbly presenting their petitions and supplications was one which emerged naturally out of that context. It evoked the familiar image of a real royal court. The original metaphor of God as "King of Kings" is biblical, but it is fleshed out with the trappings of Tudor monarchy, and from our perspective it seems to suggest arrogance and unapproachability and thereby distorts the image of God.

In the present Prayer Book there has been a move away from royal imagery, not because we no longer believe the truth which is expressed in the metaphor of divine kingship, but because the image is not congenial or immediately available to us. For us, kings and queens bring to mind either symbolic authority with little or no real power, as in most modern constitutional monarchies, tyranny, or a fairy-tale world of make believe. It is not that we cannot remythologize the image into one which we do understand, but that we must run an image like "The Lord is King"[7] through a number of mental filters before it can have the same meaning to us it had to the psalmist. In the 1979 Prayer Book, the text of the psalms was not altered to remove the image, but it is not used in prayers as frequently as in previous Prayer Books, and it is balanced with other images.

Another unquestionably biblical image is "Father." Jesus called God

"Father" and taught his disciples to do the same. It is an image of God we do not find often in the Old Testament.[8] It represents a distinctive insight into Jesus' own relationship with God and the relationship into which he calls us, his brothers and sisters, and so is by no means an image which the Church can do entirely without. But if this is the only image we use, we are apt not only to use it correctly—to name the unbegotten Source of Godhead in the other two persons of the Trinity, and to express the intensely personal relationship implied by the word "Abba" on the lips of Jesus—but also incorrectly, to invest the One who is "without body, parts, or passions"[9] with human characteristics like maleness, or a beard, or even the faults of human fathers.

Images to Enrich Liturgical Language

In a theological essay such as this one, we are free to include a footnote to explain more precisely how God is properly addressed as "Father" and of what we must be wary in doing so, just as we can explain that the use of masculine pronouns to refer to One without sex is simply grammatical convention and does not imply that the antecedent is male. Liturgy does not have this option. The words are spoken in all of their ambiguity and are not always understood in the sense that the original speaker intended. To introduce the simile of God as mother, for example, into our liturgical repertoire, not as a substitute for Father, but as a means of reminding ourselves that the attributes of divine fatherhood which we invoke are unrelated to gender or sex, is one way to attempt to manifest a more complete image of God in the liturgy. "As a mother cares for her children . . ." is certainly an image of the divine concern for us as God's children. It does not destroy the metaphor of the God and Father of our Lord Jesus Christ, but it gives us a fuller and more comprehensive picture, one more intimate and personal than "Creator."

In fact, many of the images of God used in the liturgy are "masculine," and have been historically conditioned by the patriarchal nature not only of Jewish society, but of much of Christian society. If we believe that this reflects cultural bias, and is not a part of the gospel, then the deliberate introduction of complementary "feminine" images to our worship is desirable.

This is clearly preferable to the removal of the "masculine" images, many of which are deeply embedded in both Scripture and Tradition. Removing masculine images often depersonalizes worship and theology as does the substitution of gender-free abstractions. What is needed is not the impoverishment but the enrichment of the language of prayer.

The Continuing Theological and Linguistic Exploration

When the contemporary language Rite Two was added to the Cranmerian Rite One in the 1979 Book of Common Prayer, some worshipers mourned the loss of familiar language and the images and turns of phrase with which they had become familiar over the years, and which had formed their devotional and theological thought. To them Donald Parsons, then Bishop of Quincy, addressed his devotional commentary, *The Holy Eucharist: Rite Two*, to "show that the new liturgy also has phrases which speak to our condition, [and] that it is possible to pray the Second Service too and not just suffer under it."[10] Many who considered the authorization of new alternatives imperative in 1973 do not see the force of the same argument today. The liturgy does speak to their condition, and they see no reason to introduce new language. Yet Parsons' message is intended for them also.

One of the advantages of new liturgical texts, especially those which use different images, is that they disrupt our easy familiarity with traditional phrases and challenge us to think afresh about what we really mean by the words we use. They call us not to abandon traditional faith, but to look and see what new and enriching patterns of devotion which our present rite does not afford us are offered by the supplementary texts.

The way we pray really does shape the way we think. The images and metaphors and just plain words we use in our prayer, much more than our reading of Origen or Tillich or Ricoeur or Segundo, tend to shape our faith and our thought. And since all such images are to some degree inadequate, it is wise to have a good collection of them.

The figure of Christ as the Divine Wisdom, the Hagia Sophia after whom Constantine named his great church in Constantinople, has a distinguished pedigree, but has not appeared often in liturgical prayer. A new canticle from Wisdom 10 uses this as its primary metaphor, and the joint work of Wisdom and Spirit in creation find a place in the Second Supplemental Eucharistic Prayer. The imagery from Hosea II, of God teaching Israel to walk and leading them with "cords of compassion and bands of love," is another vivid biblical image showing a different aspect of God's care for us.

Some aspects of this restoration of neglected metaphors are problematical. "Creator" is not really a synonym for "Father" any more than "creature" is a synonym for "child." God is our creator, and the creator of the entire cosmos, but we are also God's children "by adoption and grace," and that is different and speaks of a different relationship, a relationship in the Christ who called God "Abba."

The meaning of the persons of the Trinity as Father, Son, and Holy Spirit stands at the core of Christian theological tradition, and the *Gloria Patri* was painfully fought out in the patristic Church as the liturgical expression of the praise of the Triune God. The frequently-used alternative, naming the Trinity as Creator, Redeemer, and Sanctifier, appears to equate divine activities which are properly ascribed to the joint activity of the three persons, with the persons themselves. The problem, if not its solution, has been well stated by Gail Ramshaw:

> We can of course speak carefully and reverently of a God beyond sexuality, but the result of retaining masculine references for Christ is to admit a linguistic distinction which threatens the Nicean faith . . . Nicea sought to articulate the faith that God assumed humanity so that humanity might be saved. Our task is to find language which is both orthodox — which affirms "Yes we accept the Christian faith" — and kerygmatic — which suggests "This is how we say that faith in our tongue." . . . The most difficult question remains virtually unaddressed: is there a way to speak of the Trinity with more inclusive yet still orthodox terms.[11]

A most difficult problem, hinted at earlier, is the use of masculine pronouns to refer to God. To the extent that this traditional usage of English grammar causes worshipers to think of God as male or causes women to feel that their creation in God's image is being denied, it is a serious distortion of the meaning of what is being proclaimed. Fortunately, the liturgy normally addresses God directly, and second person pronouns are not gender specific in English, but the psalms, canticles, and biblical readings frequently call God "he." English, unlike many other ancient and modern languages, does not readily distinguish between grammatical gender and the sex of the antecedent. French has no difficulty with the idea that "army" and "beard" are grammatically feminine, nor German with the notion that "girl" is neuter. But English does not really have a grammatical gender, and in contemporary usage "he" is increasingly used exclusively to refer to male persons and "she" to female, while "it" implies an inanimate object. Sexual identification is so much a part of the way we experience other persons that we lack the vocabulary to speak of someone in nonsexual but personal terms. To some extent the problem can be avoided by rephrasing sentences, but eliminating the use of pronouns altogether interrupts the flow of the language.

63

In short, these supplemental prayers make a beginning at providing a fuller feast of images which may help us to rehabilitate some that have been worn out with overuse, or distorted through standing alone. Their use can be a real opportunity for spiritual growth. The Holy and Undivided Trinity whom we worship as Father, Son, and Holy Spirit is the same God to whom all of the other metaphors are applied. They do not diminish, but expand our approach to the source of all being, who is revealed to us in the vastness of interstellar space, in the complexity of sub-atomic particles, and in the warmth of human love, yet took flesh in the womb of Mary and became one of us, the divine-human person Jesus, who died for us upon the Cross and was raised again that we might share the divine life.

NOTES

1. Leonel L. Mitchell, *Liturgical Change: How Much Do We Need?* (New York: Seabury Press. 1975) pp. 9f.

2. Isaiah 55:8-9 (Canticle 10, BCP p. 86)

3. Colossians 1:15

4. Genesis 1:26

5. Marianne Micks, *The Future Present* (New York: Seabury Press. 1979) p. 159.

6. "A Prayer for the King's Majesty" at the end of Mattins in the 1662 Prayer Book.

7. Psalm 97:1; 99:1

8. It occurs in Psalm 89:26, Isaiah 63:16 and 64:8, Jeremiah 3:19, and a few other places. It is also found in prayers of the synagogue. See *Theological Dictionary of the New Testament*, edited by Gerhard Friedrich, (Grand Rapids: Eerdmans. 1967) Vol. 5, p. 978.

9. Article 1, *The Articles of Religion*, BCP p. 867

10. New York: Seabury Press. 1976, p. 2

11. Gail Ramshaw-Schmidt, "Naming the Trinity: Orthodoxy and Inclusivity," *Worship 60* (1986) pp. 491f.

Books

Guilbert, Charles Mortimer, *Words of Our Worship: A Practical Liturgical Dictionary;* The Church Hymnal Corporation, 1988

Hardesty, Nancy, A., *Inclusive Language in the Church;* John Knox Press, 1987

Hatchett, Marion J., *Commentary on the American Prayer Book;* The Seabury Press, 1980

Jasper, R.C. and David and G. J. Cuming, *Prayers and the Eucharist: Early and Reformed;* Pueblo Publishing Co., 3rd revised edition, 1987

Mitchell, Leonel L., *The Meaning of Ritual;* Morehouse-Barlow, 1977

Mitchell, Leonel L., *Planning the Church Year;* Morehouse Publishing, 1991

Mitchell, Leonel, L., *Praying Shapes Believing: A Theological Commentary on the Book of Common Prayer;* Winston Press, 1985

Morley, Janet, *All Desires Known;* Morehouse-Barlow, 1988.

Procter-Smith, Marjorie, *In Her Own Rite: Constructing Feminist Liturgical Tradition;* Arlington Nashville, 1990, Chapter Three.

Ramshaw, Gail, *Christ in Sacred Speech: The Meaning of Liturgical Language;* Fortress Press, 1986

Russell, Letty, M., *The Liberating Word;* Paulist Press, 1986

Schneiders, Sandra M., *Women and the Word;* Paulist Press, 1986

Senn, Fran C., ed., *New Eucharistic Prayers: An Ecumenical Study of Their Development and Structure;* Paulist Press, 1987

Standing Liturgical Commission, *The Occasional Papers of the Standing Liturgical Commission: Collection Number One;* The Church Hymnal Corporation, 1987

Stevick, Daniel B., *Baptismal Moments: Baptismal Meanings;* The Church Hymnal Corporation, 1987

Stevick, Daniel B., *The Crafting of Liturgy,* Church Hymnal Corporation, 1990

Stuhlman, Byron D., *Prayer Book Rubrics Expanded;* The Church Hymnal Corporation, 1987

Stuhlman, Byron D., *Eucharistic Celebration 1789-1979;* The Church Hymnal Corporation, 1988

Trible, Phyllis, *God and the Rhetoric of Sexuality;* Fortress Press, 1978

Wall, John H., Jr., *A New Dictionary for Episcopalians*; Winston Press, 1985

Weil, Louis, *Gathered to Pray: Understanding Liturgical Prayer: A Parish Life Sourcebook*; Cowley Publications and Forward Movement Publications, 1986

Weil, Louis, *Sacraments and Liturgy: The Outward Signs*; Basil Blackwell, Inc., 1983

Wren, Brian, *What language shall I borrow?: God-Talk in Worship: A male response to feminist theology*, Crossroads, 1990.

Periodicals

"Anglican Theological Review," Vol. LXXIII, No. 4 Fall, 1991. Special Issue: Language and Liturgy

Procter-Smith, Marjorie, "Liturgical Anamnesis and Women's Memory: Something Missing," pp. 405-424, *Worship*, Vol. 61, Number 5, September, 1987

Hurd, Robert L., "Complementarity: A Proposal for Liturgical Language," pp. 386-405, *Worship*, Vol. 61, Number 5, September, 1987

Westerhoff, John H., ed., *Religious Education*, Vol. 80, Number 4, Fall, 1985 (Issue on Inclusive Language)

Study Guides

A three-session study guide for adults and children was included in the Commentary of *Prayer Book Studies 30*. Though the Commentary is no longer in print, copies of the study guide are available from The Rev. Joseph Russell, Church House, 2230 Euclid Avenue, Cleveland, Ohio, 44115.

Geitz, Elizabeth, and Prescott, Margaret, "Recovering Lost Tradition: Exploring the Supplemental Liturgical Texts with a Pastoral and Historical Approach," Trinity Church, Princeton, Diocese of New Jersey, 1989

Reports

The Blue Book, 1988, Reports of the Committees, Commissions, boards, and Agencies of the General Convention of the Episcopal Church; Report of the committee on supplemental liturgical texts, page 187-198.

The Blue Book, Supplement to the Report of the Standing Liturgical Commission, 1988

The Blue Book, 1991, Report of the committee on supplemental liturgical texts, page 239-282.

Liturgical Texts for Evaluation (prepared for the Standing Liturgical Commission of the Episcopal Church, printed by The Church Hymnal Corporation, 1987.) This text was never generally available.

Supplemental Liturgical Texts; Prayer Book Studies 30, 1989. (**Out of print**)

The two lists appearing below may assist in choosing hymnody to be used in liturgies which attempt to address the issues of inclusivity.

List A is a collection of hymns which contain sexist language as far as human beings are concerned (ie, brotherhood, mankind, man, etc.)

56	105	135	383	476	558	670
78	106	158	427	489	564	717
79	107	160	445	494	565	718
87	110	179	446	497	591	719
89	119	243	450	525	605	720
94	120	244	451	531	640	
104	121	355	458	540	642	

List B contains hymns in which the God language is inclusive. These hymns contain no reference to God as "Father," "King," "He," "Lord," "Ruler," etc. The hymns with an asterisk call Jesus "Lord" in a christological sense: "Were you there when they crucified my Lord?"

6	53*	187	245*	311	420	465
7	65*	190	246*	316	422	466
8	84	194	248	317	424	468*
9*	91*	195	249	322	437*	472
12*	101*	196	251	327*	438*	473*
13*	103*	197	252	350	439*	474
16*	113	204*	256*	352	440	479
18*	138*	212	258	353	441	482*
23	140*	226	265	356	442	487
33	141*	227	279*	358	443*	498
34	142*	229	280	371	447*	508
35	150	235	284*	385	448*	509
40*	159*	269*	286	409	449*	510
41*	172*	240	299*	416	452	511
42	176	241	301	417*	453	513
51*	177	242*	310	418*	454	514

515	571*	589	601	639	682*	694
516	572*	590	602	649	683*	698
521	580	593*	603	650	684*	699
534	582	594	604	657	685	701
545	583	595	612	661*	686*	704
549	584	587*	620	673*	690	705
550	585	598*	632	675*	691	712
554	586	599	634*	676	692	713
570*	588	600	638	680	693	714
						715

APPENDIX D: Evaluation

The publishing of *Supplemental Liturgical Materials* represents a milestone in the process, ongoing for decades, through which the church is learning how to praise God fully, using the broad range of language and imagery available from scripture, tradition and the experience of the People of God. The liturgical resources contained in this volume are offered in the hope that worshipping communities throughout the church will continue to explore those elements of liturgical expression which most effectively reflect the wholeness of our experience and tradition, arriving at expressive forms which seek to incorporate the abundance of our experience of God and God's expressions of love for us.

This process of evaluation has been included in the document because a partnership between the local community and the Standing Liturgical Commission is essential if the church is to raise up for the use of the whole church the best possible liturgical language.

To help us understand your congregation's experience with these texts, and with the process in general, please send any evaluative material you produce as part of your process to The Rev. Clayton L. Morris at the Episcopal Church Center, 815 Second Avenue, New York, NY, 10017.

As you design a process of review and evaluation in your community, use any or all of the material printed here, along with whatever instruments of your own design you find helpful. It will be most helpful if your review process involves the whole congregation, especially young people and children. Younger children should be interviewed. Children old enough to participate in the process with adults should be invited to do so.

In reporting your findings to the Standing Liturgical Commission, summaries are most useful. The sheer quantity of primary data makes its use difficult because of time required for collation.

Questions for a Parish Survey

What has happened in the mind and imagination of your community as you have worshipped with these texts?

Can you identify particular images and texts in these materials which have emerged as important to your congregation?

Have new images or texts developed within your community, in response to those in this collection? If you have made editorial changes in pieces of the text, or if you have written eucharistic prayers in conjunction with "Forms for the Eucharistic Prayer" in this collection (see page 400-401 in the Book of Common Prayer), the Standing Liturgical Commission is interested in seeing your work.

What else would be important for the Standing Liturgical Commission to understand about your experience with the Supplemental Liturgical Materials?

AN OBJECTIVE SURVEY FOR CONGREGATIONAL USE

Note: The items at the left margin correspond to the main headings in the document. Each is a specific element of the liturgical text.

Participants in the survey should enter a number in each box in answer to the question the box represents. The rating scale is 1 (low) to 10 (high).

Morning and Evening Prayer	How many times have you used this text in worship?	Is this text comprehensible?	From a literary point of view, how does this text 'wear'?	Is this text spoken with ease?	Does this text evoke a 'belonging' to the body of Christ?	Is this text theologically clear?
Opening Sentences						
Absolution						
Opening versicle						
Doxology						
Antiphons						
Morning Psalm						
Evening Psalms						
Antiphons						
Canticle 12						
Canticle 15						
Canticle 16						
Canticle 18						
Canticle 21						
Additional Canticle A						
Additional Canticle B						
The Apostles Creed						

Alternative to the Salutation

Suffrages

Concluding sentence

Order of Worship
for the Evening

Opening Acclamations

Evening Psalms

Blessings

The Holy
Eucharist

Opening Acclamations

Song of Praise

Salutation

Gospel Announcement

The Nicene Creed

Prayers of the People

Absolution

The Peace

Eucharistic Prayer 1

Eucharistic Prayer 2

Forms for the Eucharistic Prayer

Memorial Acclamation A

Memorial Acclamation B

Fraction Anthems

Postcommunion Prayer

Blessings